Test Your Knowledge On The Battle Of Gettysburg

Kevin Drake

xulon PRESS

Test Your Knowledge On The Battle Of Gettysburg
by Kevin Drake

Printed in the United States of America

ISBN 9781612153636

www.xulonpress.com

This book is dedicated in memory of

MY UNCLE

MARION L. DRAKE, TROOP B
42ND SQUADRON (MECZ)
SECOND CAVALRY

WWII

SPECIAL THANKS GO OUT TO MY TWO GOOD FRIENDS FOR THEIR CONTRIBUTIONS IN MAKING THIS BOOK POSSIBLE.

GETTYSBURG LICENSED BATTLEFIELD GUIDE
REV. ROY FRAMPTON

GETTYSBURG LICENSED TOWN GUIDE
LISA SHOWER

O ne of the most gratifying aspects of writing "Test Your Knowledge on the Battle of Gettysburg" is thanking all those who have contributed to it. I thank from the bottom of my heart the following individuals and organizations:

My friends at the Gettysburg National Military Park

The Association of Licensed Battlefield Guides of Gettysburg

The Licensed Town Guides of Gettysburg

Wayne Motts, Tim Smith and the staff of the Adams County Historical Society for all their help.

When in Gettysburg, one should visit this wonderful organization located in Schmucker Hall on the campus of the Lutheran Theological Seminary.

Dr. Bradley Gottfried for his advice and encouragement at the beginning and throughout the writing of this book.

Gettysburg Licensed Town Guide Lisa Shower whose enthusiasm and passion for what the people of Gettysburg endured in July of 1863 was indispensable.

Gettysburg Licensed Battlefield Guide Roy Frampton (my battlefield mentor) and his lovely wife Lisa. Words cannot convey how much it means to me for all the time, knowledge and patience Roy has invested in me over the years.

Thank you to my mother for typing from my chicken scratch notes.

To my wife Pam, who gave me the encouragement and understanding on writing this book and always believing in me.

Kevin Drake
August 2010

INTRODUCTION

With all that is written about the American Civil War, nothing in my opinion comes close to the Battle of Gettysburg. Those three days in the summer of 1863, many brave fathers and sons of the Union and Confederacy would perform great deeds of valor. Many would survive and tell stories of the battle, but many would never return to their homes and loved ones, for they gave the ultimate sacrifice.

It is hard to describe the feeling one receives from walking the fields of this small Pennsylvania town. From the first time visitor to the ardent student of the battle, the impact of standing on the very spot where these brave men fought and died gives one a much different feeling than simply reading it in a book. From the slopes of Little Round Top where the 20th Maine charged down, to that long walk from the Virginia Monument to the Stone Wall on

Cemetery Ridge, in which many brave southern men would never return. A silent but deafening sense of honor befalls the visitor on these hallowed grounds.

I compiled this book after fourteen years and over fifty visits to Gettysburg. Upon returning to Connecticut from my first few trips, I must admit I was overwhelmed with the amount of facts and stories of the battle. I then decided to keep a notebook with me at all times and record what I had learned. "Test your Knowledge on the Battle of Gettysburg" is a result of those notes and further research on the battle. I divided the questions into three sections according to the knowledge one has of the battle. This was written to test the first time visitor to Gettysburg at Level 1 or the Civil War buff who might pick up a fact or two at Level 3. However you use this book, just please remember the brave men who fought at Gettysburg and to the courageous women of the town who tended the wounded and dying after the battle and the sacrifice they made.

John Burns Portrait Statue

LEVEL 1

PRE-BATTLE

1. The Confederate Army advancing into the North under General Robert E. Lee was known as?

   (Answer) The Army of Northern Virginia

2. What is the name of the Union Army commanded by Major General George Meade who confronted the Army of Northern Virginia at Gettysburg?

   (Answer) The Army of the Potomac

3. Was George Meade, President Abraham Lincoln's first choice to replace General Hooker as Commander of the Army of the Potomac?

(Answer) No, it was Major General John Reynolds

4. How many roads lead into Gettysburg?

(Answer) Ten

5. At the beginning of the Gettysburg battle, the two armies were moving onto the battlefield from which directions?

(Answer) The Union forces approached from the south while the Confederate forces came from the west and the north; opposite from what you would normally expect.

6. Did General Lee plan to fight at Gettysburg?

(Answer) No

7. Who informed Generals Lee and Longstreet that the Army of the Potomac had crossed the Potomac River?

(Answer) Henry Harrison

8. True or False - Henry Harrison was a captain in the Army of Northern Virginia.

   (Answer) False - He was a Confederate spy.

9. Which Confederate General was referred to as the "eyes and ears" of the Confederate Army?

   (Answer) General J.E.B. Stuart

10. What major battle had occurred in Virginia the month before the Gettysburg Campaign began?

    (Answer) Chancellorsville

11. What major cavalry battle had occurred in Virginia on June 9th at the beginning of the Gettysburg Campaign?

    (Answer) Brandy Station

12. True or False - General Lee's original plan was to fight at Cashtown not Gettysburg.

(Answer) True. He preferred Cashtown so he would have the mountains protecting his back and flanks.

13. What was General Lee's "General Order 72"?

    (Answer) It prohibited any Southern soldier from harming private property and anything taken had to be paid for in Confederate script.

14. Confederate forces had passed through Gettysburg before the major engagement began on July 1st, on what date and led by whom?

    (Answer) June 26, 1863 led by General Jubal Early

15. True or False - At approximately 3:00 a.m. on June 28, General Meade was awaken out of a deep sleep and thought he was being arrested.

    (Answer) True, but he was informed that he was now commanding the Army of the Potomac and not being arrested.

16. On July 1st, what health issues plagued General Lee?

   (Answer) He suffered from the after effects of a heart attack and had a case of dysentery.

17. What does the "E" stand for in the name of Robert E. Lee?

   (Answer) Edward

The First Day of the Battle of Gettysburg: July 1,1863

18. Abner Doubleday, who assumed command of the Union First Corps at Gettysburg, is the disputed founder of what sport?

   (Answer) Baseball

19. Who was the first soldier killed in the Gettysburg Campaign?

   (Answer) George Washington Sandoe

20. On July 1st, the first shot of the Battle of Gettysburg was fired around what time?

   (Answer) 7:30 A.M.

21. Who fired the first shot of the Battle of Gettysburg?

   (Answer) Second Lieutenant Marcellus Jones, 8th Illinois Cavalry

22. True or False - Confederate President Jefferson Davis had a nephew in command of a brigade at Gettysburg.

   (Answer) True - He was General Joseph Davis.

23. The morning of July 1ˢ Confederate forces first encountered a Union Cavalry Division commanded by whom?

   (Answer) Brig. General John Buford

24. General John Buford had what two difficulties in the placement of his cavalry the morning of July 1?

(Answer) *(1) He had approximately 2,800 Cavalry spread out approximately seven miles, flank to flank.*

(2) One of four men in each regiment would have to hold the horses once they dismounted and go to the rear, taking them away from the fighting.

25. Who had the distinction of being the first Union casualty of the battle?

(Answer) Private John E. Weaver, 3rd Indiana Cavalry.

26. How far from Gettysburg was the closest Union Infantry Corps on the early morning of July 1?

(Answer) The First Corps about 4.5 miles away.

27. Although outnumbered, what advantage did the Union Cavalry have over the Confederate Infantry?

(Answer) *The Union wielded single shot breech loaders while the Confederates relied on muzzle loaded muskets.*

28. What Confederate Division commander advanced against Gettysburg the morning of July 1?

    (Answer) *General Henry Heth*

29. Confederate General Henry Heth sent General James Archer's Brigade forward into Herbst Woods to dislodge dismounted Union Cavalry but who did they run into?

    (Answer) *Infantry from the Union First Corps.*

30. How did General Archer's Brigade refer to the Union First Corps "Iron Brigade"?

    (Answer) *"Those Damn Black Hatted Fella's".*

31. Who commanded the Eleventh Corps at the start of the battle?

(Answer) Major General Oliver O. Howard

32. Just before General Reynolds was shot, what did he shout to the advancing Iron Brigade?

    (Answer) "Forward men, forward for God's sake, and drive those fellows out of the woods."

33. What nationality made up a large portion of the Union Eleventh Corps?

    (Answer) German

34. Did General Alfred Iverson personally lead his North Carolina Brigade against the Union Forces on Oak Ridge?

    (Answer) No, he stayed on Oak Hill in the rear and observed.

35. After Major General Reynolds was killed, who commanded the First Corps?

    (Answer) Major General Abner Doubleday

36. Confederate General Archer had what distinction regarding his capture by the Iron Brigade?

    (Answer) He was the first Confederate General taken prisoner in action since General Lee assumed command of the Confederate Army.

37. Upon seeing Confederate General James Archer being taken to the rear, General Abner Doubleday knowing General Archer before the war said "Archer, I'm glad to see you". What was General Archer's reply?

    (Answer) "Well, I am not glad to see you by damn sight."

38. What was the rally point that the Union First and Eleventh Corps retreated to at the end of the first day's battle?

    (Answer) Cemetery Hill

39. True or False - General Richard Ewell and General Stonewall Jackson were successful in capturing the town of Gettysburg on July 1.

(Answer) False - Stonewall Jackson had previously been mortally wounded, and he was not at the battle. General Ewell replaced him.

40. At 7:00 P.M. on July 1, who controlled the town of Gettysburg?

    (Answer) The Confederates

41. What was General Lee's ambiguous instruction to General Ewell on attacking Cemetery Hill on July 1?

    (Answer) "Take that hill if practicable."

42. Did General Ewell take Cemetery Hill on July 1?

    (Answer) No, he did not take the hill.

43. A dead Union soldier holding a picture of his three children was found on the corner of Stratton and York Streets. After printing the picture in the newspaper, he was identified. Who was he?

    (Answer) He was Sgt. Amos Humiston, 154th New York.

The Second Day of the Battle of Gettysburg: July 2, 1863

44. The Union Army's battle line on July 2 resembled what?

    (Answer) A fishhook.

45. What Corps Commander said "I will be damned if I take the responsibility for this fight."

    (Answer) Union General Henry Slocum

46. What Union General ordered his men to build breast-works on Culp's Hill?

    (Answer) General George S. Greene

47. Who earned the nickname "The Savior of Little Round Top" securing the high ground on the Union flank on July 2?

    (Answer) Chief Engineer - Brigadier General Gouverneur K. Warren

48. Who positioned his brigade, placing the 20th Maine at the far end of the Union flank on Little Round Top?

(Answer) Colonel Strong Vincent

49. Who commanded the 20th Maine regiment?

(Answer) Colonel Joshua Chamberlain

50. What Major General commanding the Union Third Corps, not liking his position, moved his troops forward without orders from General Meade?

(Answer) Major General Daniel Sickles

51. Did General Meade agree that General Sickles was justified by moving his command forward?

(Answer) No, he was furious.

52. What Union Colonel, commanding the 140th New York was shot through the neck on Little Round Top while

leading a counter-charge against the 4th and 5th Texas Regiments?

(Answer) Colonel Patrick O'Rorke

53. Colonel Patrick O'Rorke graduated first in his class at West Point. Which fellow Union General finished last in that same class?

(Answer) Brigadier General George A. Custer

54. True or False. - Confederate troops from Alabama, Texas, Mississippi, Georgia, attacked Devil's Den.

(Answer) False. Mississippi troops did not fight at Devil's Den.

55. What Brigadier Commander wore a red bandana traditionally into battle but at Gettysburg wore a black one - a premonition of his own death in the Wheatfield?

(Answer) Colonel Edward Cross

56. On what farm was General Sickles wounded on July 2?

(Answer) The Trostle Farm

57. Did General Sickles lose an arm or leg or both on July 2?

(Answer) His right leg only

58. What did an annoyed General Lee say when Confederate General J.E.B. Stuart arrived on the afternoon of July 2?

(Answer) "Well General, you are here at last."

59. According to legend when carried off the battlefield on a stretcher, what did General Sickles do to show his men he was still alive?

(Answer) He put a cigar in his mouth.

60. What Brigadier General from Mississippi smashed through Union soldiers in the Peach Orchard?

(Answer) Brigadier General William Barksdale

61. What did General Longstreet say about his offensive on July 2?

(Answer) "It was the best three hours of fighting by any troops on any battlefield."

The Third Day of the Battle of Gettysburg: July 3, 1863

62. True or False - General James Longstreet did not want to assault the center of the Union line which is known today as "Pickett's Charge" on July 3.

   (Answer) True

63. Where on Cemetery Ridge is it believed that General Lee wanted to concentrate his attack?

   (Answer) The copse of trees at the Angle.

64. Will today's visitor to the copse of trees walk among the original trees that witnessed the battle?

(Answer) No, unfortunately they are not original.

65. At the time of the bombardment, did the fighting on Culps Hill begin or was it finished?

    (Answer) It had finished.

66. Did Union General Hunt handle his artillery superbly or poorly in counter fire and tactic to E. Porter Alexander's cannonade?

    (Answer) Superbly

67. True or False - Confederate General Pickett was killed on July 3 in the charge that bears his name.

    (Answer) False, he was not killed but held a deep resentment toward General Lee.

68. Did General Lee order General Ewell to co-ordinate his attack on Culp's Hill with General Longstreet's attack?

    (Answer) Yes

69. Did General George Pickett and General Jeb Stuart arrive at Gettysburg on July 2 or July 3?

   (Answer) July 2, 1863 - the second day of the battle.

70. What did General Lee tell General Longstreet when he suggested the move around Meade's left?

   (Answer) "The enemy is there General Longstreet and I am going to strike him there."

71. What was the highest recorded temperature on July 3?

   (Answer) 87 degrees and humid

72. Did the Confederate artillery bombardment from approximately 1:00 P.M. to 3:00 P.M. have the effect and devastation on the Union line that the Confederates desired?

   (Answer) No, they overshot their targets, hitting the reserves and medical personnel in the rear.

73. Did General Lee intend his artillery to move forward with the infantry during Pickett's Charge?

    (Answer) Yes

74. What Confederate Brigade General when charging the Angle, stuck his hat at the point of his sword yelling "Give them the cold steel, boys!".

    (Answer) General Lewis Armistead

75. What did General Lee say after witnessing the returning men from the failed charge?

    (Answer) "It's all my fault."

76. Did General Lee order the town of Gettysburg to be burned while the Confederates retreated?

    (Answer) No.

77. Who was the Corps Commander of the Union Cavalry at Gettysburg?

(Answer) Major General Alfred Pleasonton

78. Who was the Division Commander of the Confederate Cavalry at Gettysburg?

(Answer) General J.E.B. Stuart

79. Appearing at the head of the 7th Michigan Cavalry, General George Custer yelled what to his men?

(Answer) "Come on, you Wolverines!"

POST-BATTLE

80. When did General Lee start his retreat back to Virginia?

(Answer) The evening of July 4^t, 1863.

81. Was it a clear sky or pouring rain on July 4, 1863?

(Answer) Pouring rain

82. How long was General Lee's ambulance wagon train back to Virginia?

    (Answer) Approximately 17 miles

83. Would General Meade order a full force attack against General Lee before he retreated into Virginia?

    (Answer) No, only some skirmishes would take place before General Lee crossed the Potomac.

MISCELLANEOUS

84. How many rings are found on a Confederate Minie Ball?

    (Answer) Two

85. How many rings are found on a Union Minie Ball?

    (Answer) Three

86. Beside Solid Shot, name three other types of artillery rounds.

    (Answer) 1) Case Shot 2) Shell 3) Canister

87. Union artillery batteries were organized into units called what?

    (Answer) Brigades

88. Confederate artillery batteries were organized into units called what?

    (Answer) Battalions

89. True or False - The green cannons seen on the battlefield today were colored green for camouflage purposes.

    (Answer) False, the green color results from oxidized bronze.

90. A Confederate breech loading cannon, manufactured in England and used at Gettysburg was called what?

(Answer) Whitworth

91. What is the name of General Lee's horse that he rode on July 3rd?

(Answer) Traveller

92. What was the name of General Meade's horse?

(Answer) Old Baldy

93. What is the name of the dog located on the front of the 11th Pennsylvania monument?

(Answer) Sallie - She was the mascot of the 11th Pennsylvania.

94. After the battle, who photographed all the dead horses on the Trostle Farm?

(Answer) Timothy O'Sullivan

95. According to the 1860 census, what was the population of the town of Gettysburg?

  (Answer) 2,400

96. How many Medals of Honor were awarded for the Gettysburg Campaign?

  (Answer) Sixty-two for the battle, seventy-one for the campaign.

97. True or False - Women fought in the battle dressed as men.

  (Answer) True

98. At Gettysburg, what color flag was most commonly placed in areas used as hospitals?

  (Answer) Red, but a Union regulation hospital flag is yellow with a green letter H in the center.

99. How old was John Burns at the Battle of Gettysburg?

    (Answer) Sixty-nine years old.

100. Did he fight in any war prior to The Civil War?

    (Answer) Yes, the War of 1812.

101. Father James Burlando and a group of twelve Roman Catholic Sisters who took baskets of bandages, food and other necessities and were among the first outside of Gettysburg to provide help after the battle. What was this group of Catholic Sisters called?

    (Answer) The Order of the Daughters of Charity from Emmitsburg, Maryland.

102. Which Gettysburg heroine dug over one hundred graves with the help of her elderly father despite being six months pregnant?

    (Answer) Elizabeth Thorn

103. Which large hotel was located at the intersection of Chambersburg and Washington Streets at the time of the battle and was General Buford's headquarters on June 30,1863?

(Answer) The Eagle Hotel

104. Prior to the battle, local residents used the 17 acre woodlot south of McPherson's Farm for what purpose?

(Answer) This area was used as the town's picnic grounds.

105. What is the oldest house in Gettysburg today?

(Answer) The Dobbin House, 1776.

106. Who owned the building which today is called "General Lee's Headquarters" during the battle?

(Answer) Congressman Thaddeus Stevens

107. Who lived at that house during the battle?

(Answer) Widow Mary Thompson

108. Who is the founder of the Lutheran Theological Seminary?

(Answer) Samuel Simon Schmucker

109. A resident of Gettysburg kept accurate weather records during the three-day battle, who was he?

(Answer) Professor Michael Jacobs

110. Who was the only Gettysburg civilian killed during the three-day battle?

(Answer) Jennie Wade

111. True or False - Jennie Wade was killed in her house while baking bread.

(Answer) False - She was in her sister's house baking bread.

112. At what time was the train expected to travel down the railroad cut on July 1 and would it have traveled through the fighting?

    (Answer) There was no train because the track was not laid at the time of battle.

113. In 1939, what family opened the Electric Map?

    (Answer) The Rosensteel Family

114. True or False - After the Civil War there was a trolley running through Devil's Den as well as a dance hall and photo studio.

    (Answer) True

115. What monument is sculpted as a tree complete with a birds nest containing a mother and her young?

(Answer) 90th PA

116. What is the oldest regimental monument?

(Answer) The 2nd Massachusetts Monument.

117. Who sculpted the Virginia Monument?

(Answer) F. William Sievers

118. What is the unofficial oldest monument at Gettysburg?

(Answer) The Minnesota Urn

119. Where is the Minnesota Urn monument located?

(Answer) The Soldiers National Cemetery

120. What is the largest and most elaborate monument on the battlefield honoring the men who fought there?

(Answer) The Pennsylvania State Monument

121. What Catholic priest stood on a rock and pronounced absolution to members of the Irish Brigade as well as other soldiers of different denominations on July 2? His monument marks the spot of his speech.

(Answer) Father William Corby

122. What regimental chaplain was shot on the steps of Christ Lutheran Church on July 1st because he was carrying a ceremonial sword?

(Answer) Horatio Howell

123. Which U.S. President dedicated the Eternal Light Peace Memorial?

(Answer) Franklin D. Roosevelt

124. Is John Burns buried in the Soldiers National Cemetery or Evergreen Cemetery?

(Answer) Evergreen Cemetery

125. Who was the Governor of Pennsylvania who autho-rized the establishment of the Gettysburg Soldiers National Cemetery?

    (Answer) Governor Andrew Curtin

126. Who was the Gettysburg attorney, appointed by Governor Andrew Curtin to establish the Gettysburg Soldiers National Cemetery?

    (Answer) David Wills

127. Who supervised the disinterment of the battlefield graves and the re-interment of the bodies in the Soldiers National Cemetery?

    (Answer) Samuel Weaver

128. Was Abraham Lincoln the keynote speaker at the dedi-cation ceremony?

    (Answer) No, it was Edward Everett.

129. Was the speaker platform where President Lincoln delivered the Gettysburg Address in the Soldiers National Cemetery or Evergreen Cemetery?

(Answer) Evergreen Cemetery.

130. True or False - Jennie Wade, John Burns, and Wesley Culp are all buried in Evergreen Cemetery.

(Answer) False - The grave of Wesley Culp remains unknown.

131. How old was President Lincoln when he gave the Gettysburg Address?

(Answer) Fifty-four

132. How many original copies of the Gettysburg Address exist today?

(Answer) Five

133. At the 75th Reunion of the Battle, 1800 veterans attended. What was the average age?

    (Answer) Ninety-four years old

134. After the battle, Fredrick Biesecker won the contract for exhuming and re-interment of the dead Union bodies. What was the winning bid?

    (Answer) One dollar and fifty-nine cents ($1.59) per body.

135. On what date did President Lincoln deliver the Gettysburg Address?

    (Answer) November 19, 1863

136. Does the memorial erected in 1912 to commemorate Lincoln's Gettysburg Address mark the spot where he gave the speech?

    (Answer) No

137. The iron fence that separates the National Cemetery from Evergreen Cemetery came from where?

(Answer) The fence came from Lafayette Square near the White House, Washington, D.C.

138. True or False - The official code of the equestrian statues on the battlefield is two (2) hoofs off the base indicates death of the rider, one hoof off the base indicates the rider was wounded and no hoofs off the base, means the rider survived unharmed.

(Answer) False, there is no official code of equestrian statues.

139. What is hardtack?

(Answer) A cracker made of flour, salt and water that after time would become rock hard. Some were infested with small bugs and men would call them "worm castles".

140. What is referred to a "skillygallee?

> *(Answer) Salted pork with crumbled hardtack in a mixture and fried.*

141. What is "coosh"?

> *(Answer) A Confederate dish of bacon fat mixed with some water and corn meal and cooked in a pan, or rolled on a ramrod, over a fire.*

142. What is a haversack?

> *(Answer) A bag slung over the shoulder used to transport personal items and daily rations carried by foot soldiers.*

143. What was carried by some soldiers known as a "housewife"?

> *(Answer) A name for a soldier's kit containing the essentials needed to mend uniforms and other clothing.*

"WHO AM I?"

(Name the person, or object from the description)

I graduated West Point in 1844. I was given the nickname "The Superb" for my performance in the Peninsula Campaign. I took command of the First, Third and Eleventh Corps at Gettysburg on the afternoon of July 1, even though General Howard outranked me. I was wounded on July 3 along with my good friend Confederate General Armistead on the same field.

Who Am I?

Winfield Scott Hancock

I was a West Pointer and a veteran of the Mexican War. I gave Robert E. Lee fits as I blasted his frontal assaults on Mavern Hill. I co-wrote the Army manual of artillery used by both North and South. I was almost injured by a stampede of frightened cattle at Gettysburg.

Who Am I?

Henry Hunt

I was a West Pointer and fought in the Mexican War. I led the massive counterblow that decimated John Pope at Second Manassas. I was referred to as "Old Pete" although Lee called me his "old war horse". I would have preferred to move between the Union army and Washington instead of fighting at Gettysburg. I was a groomsman at General Grant's wedding.

Who Am I?

James Longstreet

I was sixty-nine (69) years old at the time of the battle when I joined the fighting on July 1. I was a veteran of the War of 1812 and former constable. Don't think much of the citizens of town for not taking up arms like I did with my flintlock. I was wounded three times. President Lincoln and I attended

church together for a political meeting after the battle when he came to town to deliver the Gettysburg Address.
Who Am I?

John Burns

"WHO AM I?"

I graduated second in my class at West Point. My father was called "Light Horse Harry" and fought in the Revolutionary War. I turned down the post of Commander of the Army defending Washington in 1861. Instead, I joined the Confederacy and in 1862 I took command of the Army of Northern Virginia that would fight here at Gettysburg.

Who Am I?

Robert E. Lee

I am fluent in several languages and I was a lawyer and politician from New York. I did not attend West Point or even graduate college. I am the first person in U.S. Legal History to successfully plead "temporary insanity". I commanded a Corps at Gettysburg and lost my leg on July 2. When asked for the location of my monument here at Gettysburg, I responded "the whole damn battlefield is my monument."

Who Am I?

Daniel Sickles

Born in Pennsylvania, at seventeen years old, I applied and was accepted to West Point, where I trained in artillery. Prior to fighting at Gettysburg I was captured and exchanged. I refused the command of the Army of the Potomac when it was offered. At Gettysburg, I was a Wing Commander and committed to fight outside of town but it cost me my life.

Who Am I?

John Reynolds

I am a native of Virginia. I attended West Point with future Generals Hooker and Sedgwick. I am told I am selfish and sarcastic and fellow Cadet Lewis Armistead even broke a plate over my head at West Point. I love to chew tobacco and couldn't care less if someone didn't like it. General Lee called me "my bad old man". I was already in Gettysburg on June 26 and when I left it I had to turn back and smash those Yankees on the afternoon of July 1.

Who Am I?

Jubal Early

HOW DID YOU DO? LEVEL 1

(A)   15 or less questions answered incorrectly

Rank: Colonel

GREAT JOB! IT'S AN HONOR TO MEET YOU, SIR!!

(B) **38 or less questions answered incorrectly**

<u>Rank</u>:   Major

NOT BAD. PLEASED TO MEET YOU, SIR!!

(C) **39 or more questions answered incorrectly**

<u>Rank</u>:   Private

YOU NEED TO HIT THEM BOOKS!'

BUT FIRST, COOK NEEDS SOME HELP WITH

SOME POTATOES.

Whitworth on Oak Hill

LEVEL 2

PRE-BATTLE

1. True or False - One of General Lee's hopes was by moving the Army of Northern Virginia north, it would relieve pressure on Vicksburg, feed his army and frighten Northerners to sue for peace.

    (Answer) True

2. The Confederate government still held the hope that which two European countries would assist the Confederate cause?

    (Answer) England and/or France.

3. General Lee's three Confederate Corps commanders moved from their encampment in Virginia to begin the northern invasion in what order?

(Answer) Ewell's corps, Longstreet's corps and lastly the corps of A.P. Hill.

4. What Pennsylvania Volunteer Militia was sent to Gettysburg on June 26 to defend the town?

(Answer) The 26th[tt] Pennsylvania Emergency Militia.

5. What was General A. P. Hill's skeptical response to General Pettigrew's report that he had a run in with the Union Cavalry and advance units of the Army of the Potomac on June 30?

(Answer) It was a mere "detachment of observation" and not the Army of the Potomac, nothing more than a "home guard or militia".

6. General Heth also very skeptical of General Pettigrew's report, asked General A. P. Hill if he had any problems with him taking his division to Gettysburg the next morning. What was General A. P. Hill's response?

(Answer) "None in the world,"

7. On June 30, where was General Ewell?

(Answer) Carlisle

8. Union General John Buford was born in which state?

(Answer) Kentucky

9. On July 1, Cyrus James of the 9th New York Cavalry was shot out of his saddle, but his foot got caught in his stirrup, whereupon his horse dragged him into the town. What Gettysburg civilian released him by cutting him loose?

(Answer) John Burns

10. Union General George G. Meade was born in which state?

    (Answer) He was not born in the United States, but in Spain.

11. Why did this campaign become a very personal affair for General John Reynolds?

    (Answer) His hometown of Lancaster was only 50 miles away to the east.

12. Was Edward McPherson present on his farm at the time of the battle?

    (Answer) No, he was in Washington.

13. Who was on the Edward McPherson Farm at the time of the battle?

    (Answer) John Slentz and his family who were Edward McPherson's tenants.

July 1, 1863

14. Name the five regiments that made up the Iron Brigade.

(Answer) The 2nd, 6th, 7th Wisconsin, 19th Indiana and the 24th Michigan.

15. Who commanded the Union's Iron Brigade?

(Answer) Brigadier General Solomon Meredith

16. What was the nickname of the 14th Brooklyn Regiment (84th New York)?

(Answer) "Red Legged Devils"

17. Who was known as the "Boy Colonel"?

(Answer) Henry King Burgwyn was the youngest colonel at Gettysburg, sadly he would be killed on July 1 at the age of twenty-one years.

18. What regiment did Confederate Colonel Henry King Burgwyn command?

    (Answer) 26th North Carolina

19. What heroic Color Sergeant was shot down shaking his fist at approaching Confederates on July I, many Confederates, even General A. P. Hill felt remorse about killing this brave soldier?

    (Answer) Color Sergeant Ben Crippen 143th Pennsylvania.

20. Was there a light rain on the early morning of July 1, 1863?

    (Answer) Yes

21. Union General John Reynolds was Wing Commander of what three Corps?

    (Answer) The First Corps, Third Corps, and Eleventh Corps.

22`. What were the Union Pioneer's responsibilities on July 1?

(Answer) *To knock down fences and obstacles hindering the advancing infantry.*

23. When General Abner Doubleday took command of the First Corps, who took command of his old Division (Third Division First Corps)?

(Answer) *Brigadier General Thomas Rowley*

24. What stream did General Archer's Brigade cross as they advanced up the slopes of McPherson's Ridge?

(Answer) *Willoughby Run*

25. How many times did the flag of the 24th Michigan fall on July 1, as the color bearers were successively shot down?

(Answer) *Fourteen*

26. On July 1, who was the highest ranking Confederate officer captured?

     (Answer) General James Archer

27. After arriving with his Eleventh Corps, where does Union General O. O. Howard witness the retreat of General Cutler's men?

     (Answer) From the roof of the Fahnestock Mercantile Building in town.

28. In his report, who does General Howard hold responsible for the collapse of the Union First Corps?

     (Answer) General Abner Doubleday

29. Name the Colonel of the 6th Wisconsin who took 250 Confederate prisoners in the railroad cut?

     (Answer) Colonel Rufus Dawes

30. On July 1, John Burns approached the 151st Pennsylvania and asked permission of its Colonel to fight alongside them. What was he wearing?

> *(Answer) He wore a dark, swallow-tailed coat, buff color vest, dark trousers and a high silk hat.*

31. At what time of day on July 1 was there a lull in the fighting which allowed both sides to regroup and reorganize?

> *(Answer) Approximately 11:00 A.M.*

32. After General Howard took command of the Army at Gettysburg, where did he set up his headquarters?

> *(Answer) Cemetery Hill*

33. Was the house Abraham Spangler and his family lived in near Culps Hill or Willoughby's Run?

> *(Answer) Willoughby's Run*

34. Did General Wadsworth attend Yale, Harvard, both or no university at all?

    (Answer) He attended both, Harvard and Yale

35. Which regiment of Union General Lysander Cutler's brigade suffered the highest casualty rate?

    (Answer) 147th New York

36. What regiment was ordered by General Robinson to "hold at any cost" and were sacrificed while allowing others in the First Corps to escape?

    (Answer) The 16th Maine

37. Who commanded the 16th Maine?

    (Answer) Colonel Charles W. Tilden

38. The 151st Pennsylvania, Company D was composed of many teachers and students from Lost Creek Academy,

McAllisterville, Juniata County. Who was the school prin-
cipal at the same school and commanded the regiment?

(Answer) Colonel George McFarland

39. What injury did General Gabriel Paul sustain and what
regiment was he in the rear of when it happened?

> *(Answer) He was shot through the eyes and blinded
> and was in the area behind the 104th New
> York.*

40. What Colonel under General John Buford deployed three
Cavalry regiments, opened fire, causing Confederate
troops under Brigadier General James Lane to form
Napoleonic squares and draw them away from the
assault on the Seminary line on the afternoon of July 1?

(Answer) Colonel William Gamble

41. What was the first regiment of the Eleventh Corps to
deploy onto the battlefield?

(Answer) The 45th New York

42. What was the fate of Lieutenant Colonel Douglas Fowler when he was moving the 17th Connecticut in position on (present day) "Barlow's Knoll"?

(Answer) He was decapitated.

43. What southern brigade had the honor of entering the town of Gettysburg first?

(Answer) Colonel Perrin's brigade from South Carolina

44. What three regiments did Colonel Charles Coster take to the Brickyard to cover the retreat of his comrades?

(Answer) The 134th New York, 27th Pennsylvania and 154th New York.

45. Who owned the Brickyard located along North Stratton Street?

(Answer) John Kuhns

July 2

46. How old was Union General George S. Greene at the time of the battle?

    (Answer) He was sixty-two years old.

47. On July 2, did most of the Twelfth Corps help General Greene defend Culps Hill?

    (Answer) No, around 6:00 P.M. the Twelfth Corps was removed from Culps Hill and rushed to bolster the left end of the Union line.

48. About what time did the Twelfth Corps return to Culps Hill on July 2?

    (Answer) Approximately 11:00 P.M.

49. Having witnessed such heavy fighting, the strip of land between the base of Little Round Top and the Wheatfield earned what nickname?

(Answer) The Valley of Death

50. How did Union Captain Bruce Ricketts describe the resistance offered by the 54th and 68th New York against Confederate Colonel Isaac Avery's brigade?

> *(Answer) Captain Ricketts lamented "It was cowardly and disgraceful in the extreme."*

51. As the 20th Connecticut advanced forward they were hit by friendly fire from their own batteries. What did Lieutenant Colonel William Wooster say in a message sent to the battery commander?

> *(Answer) "If it happens again, I will pull my men out of line, face them about and charge his own guns."*

52. During the Union shelling, what unfortunate Private from the 20th Connecticut had both arms blown off by this friendly fire?

> *(Answer) Private George W. Warner*

53. What regiment would hold the extreme right of the Union line of July 2 at 7:00 P.M. on Culps Hill?

(Answer) The 137th New York

54. Name Union General John Caldwell's Brigade Commanders at the beginning of the Battle of the Wheatfield.

(Answer) First Brigade: Colonel Edward Cross
Second Brigade: Colonel Patrick Kelly
Third Brigade: General Samuel Zook
Forth Brigade: Colonel John R. Brooke

55. Of these four Commanders, who commanded the "Irish Brigade"?

(Answer) Colonel Patrick Kelly

56. This 4th Michigan Colonel was bayoneted in the Wheatfield trying to save his regiments colors?

(Answer) Colonel Harrison Jeffords

57. Name the five regiments in the Irish Brigade.

>   *(Answer) 1) 28th MASS*
>
>   *2) 63rd NY*
>
>   *3) 69th NY*
>
>   *4) 88th NY*
>
>   *5) 116th PA*

58. Name the four regiments under Union Colonel Strong Vincent's Brigade and who commanded each regiment.

>   *(Answer) 1) 16th Michigan - Lt. Colonel Norval Welch*
>
>   *2) 44th New York - Colonel James Rice*
>
>   *3) 83rd Pennsylvania - Captain Orpheus Woodward*
>
>   *4) 20th Maine - Colonel Joshua Chamberlain*

59. How long was it after the 20th Maine was positioned on Little Round Top that they were attacked?

>   *(Answer) Approximately ten minutes*

60. Who commanded the 5th U.S. Battery D and was killed by a sharpshooter in the defense of Little Round Top?

   (Answer) First Lieutenant Charles Hazlett

61. Name Colonel Joshua Chamberlain's two brothers and where did each serve at Gettysburg?

   (Answer) Tom - 20th Maine, John – United States Christian Commission.

62. Who commanded the 1st Minnesota when General Hancock ordered it to charge?

   (Answer) Colonel William Colvill

63. What Division Commander took the standard on the side of Little Round Top and "yelled forward Reserves" as he charged down the hill?

   (Answer) General Samuel Crawford

64. Who commanded the 9th Massachusetts Light Artillery during their desperate stand against the Confederate troops under Generals Kershaw and Barksdale?

(Answer) Captain John Bigelow

65. The 9th Massachusetts Battery had participated in how many other battles before Gettysburg?

(Answer) None, it was their first battle.

66. This brave bugler of the 9th Massachusetts Light Artillery helped save his Commander and was awarded the Congressional Medal of Honor. Who was he?

(Answer) Bugler Charles Reed

67. Why was Confederate General Ambrose Wright furious after his failed assault upon Cemetery Ridge on the evening of July 2?

(Answer) Brigadier General Carnot Posey and William Mahone never advanced to support him.

68. On the evening of July 2, General Meade held a Council of War at which Gettysburg resident's home?

    (Answer) The Leister House

69. What did Gouverneur Warren do during General Meade's Council of War?

    (Answer) He slept in the corner after getting wounded at Little Round Top.

70. At that Council of War, Chief of Staff Major General Daniel Butterfield asked to vote on three issues. What were they?

    (Answer) 1) Should the Army remain where it was or move closer to its base of operations?
    2) If they were to stay, should they attack or remain on the defense?

3) If they remain on defense, how long should the Army wait for an attack?

71. True or False - General Lee's Council of War on July 2 consisted of Generals James Longstreet, A.P. Hill and Ambrose Wright.

(Answer) False

July 3

72. What time did the fighting on Culps Hill resume on July 3?

(Answer) Approximately 5:00 A.M.

73. Who wrote the letter of introduction to West Point for George Pickett?

(Answer) Abraham Lincoln

74. Name General George Pickett's three Brigade Commanders who made the charge on July 3, 1863.

(Answer) General Lewis Armistead, General Richard Garnett and General James Kemper.

75. Out of these three generals, how many returned uninjured?

(Answer) None. Garnett was killed instantly, Kemper and Armistead both received serious wounds

- Armistead would die days later, only Kemper would survive.

76. Which two Brigades of General Anderson's Division would form on Pickett's right?

(Answer) The Brigades of General Wilcox and General Perry (under Colonel Lang).

77. Which two Brigades of General Anderson's division, who previously suffered the least amount of losses, were not used during Pickett's charge?

(Answer) General Mahone's and General Posey's Brigades.

78. Who took the brunt of the casualties during the bombardment of July 3?

(Answer) The Union artillery reserve, supply and medical personnel, supply and ammunition wagons all held in reserve. This was

due to the Confederates overshooting their intended targets.

79. During the bombardment, where did General Meade's staff move their headquarters so that they were out of the range of fire?

(Answer) They moved to General Slocum's head-quarters on Powers Hill.

80. During the bombardment, General Hancock rode along the Union lines with the Second Corps flag behind him. What was his response when told "not to risk your life this way"?

(Answer) General Hancock replied "There are times when a Corps Commander's life does not count."

81. When the hand to hand fighting commenced at the Angle, Union troops who were unable to reach the Confederates through the crowd resorted to using what as weapons?

(Answer) Union soldiers hurled rocks over their own troops into the Confederates.

82. How did General Judson Kilpatrick try to justify his orders that sent Brigadier General Elon Farnsworth to his death?

    (Answer) General Kilpatrick thought General Meade had ordered a general counterattack from Cemetery Hill and wanted to cooperate on the south flank.

83. Which regiment went to court to get permission to have their monument placed at the stone wall of the Angle?

    (Answer) 72nd Pennsylvania

MISCELLANEOUS

84. When the statue of John Buford on the Chambersburg Pike was dedicated on July 1, 1895, what symbolic gesture did Major Calef perform to the four ordinance rifle tubes at the base of the monument?

    (Answer) He symbolically spiked the four tubes.

85. What is the full name of the inventor of the minie ball?

    (Answer) Claude-Etienne Minie

86. True or False - The Confederate Army took some citizens of Gettysburg south as captives.

    (Answer) True

87. What building was the largest mercantile business in town and was an observation point on July 1, 1863.

    (Answer) The Fahnestock Brothers General Merchandise Store.

88. Which church in town was referred to as the college church?

   (Answer) Christ Lutheran Church on Chambersburg Street.

89. Who was the Burgess (Mayor) in Gettysburg at the time of the battle?

   (Answer) Robert Martin

90. What was the profession of Robert Martin?

   (Answer) He ran a tailor shop with his father by the Square in town.

91. Since Robert Martin, the Burgess of Gettysburg, left town prior to the arrival of Confederate General Jubal Early on June 26, who was sent for to receive General Early's demands on the town?

   (Answer) The president of the Town Council - David Kendlehart

92. Charles Tyson's Photography Studio was located on what street?

    (Answer) York Street

93. Colonel Charles Wheelock of the 97th N.Y. Volunteers was captured in which resident's home on July 1st.

    (Answer) Elias Sheads

94. General Alexander Schimmelfenning hid in a wooden culvert over a water course on the property of Henry Garlach. Was he captured?

    (Answer) No, he evaded capture.

95. This Michigan Colonel was captured on July 1, but not before giving his diary to Mary McAllister in her home for safekeeping and would later be taken prisoner.

    (Answer) Colonel Henry Murrow, 24th Michigan

96. During the retreat through town on July 1, a Major from the 2nd Wisconsin would take refuge in the home of Mary McAllister. Fearing his capture, he tried to hide in her chimney until Colonel Henry Murrow told him "you will not, it would endanger this family", gritting his teeth in anger, he crawled out of the chimney and was captured. Who was he?

(Answer) Lieutenant Dennis Burke Dailey - 2nd Wisconsin

97. What was so important about the sword carried by Lieutenant Dailey?

(Answer) It was the sword Confederate General James Archer had surrendered to him.

98. Did the Confederates recapture General Archer's sword along with Lieutenant Dailey?

(Answer) No, Mary McAllister hid the sword.

99. Did Colonel Murrow and Lieutenant Dailey escape when captured by Confederate soldiers?

> *(Answer) Yes. Colonel Murrow disguised himself as a Confederate surgeon and escaped when it was dark. Major Dailey escaped when his guard fell asleep.*

100. The Excelsior Brigade monument pays tribute to the 70th, 71st, 72nd, 73rd, and 74th New York infantry regiments. The monument contains an empty pedestal, which was intended to hold a bust of what Union General?

> *(Answer) Daniel Sickles*

101. Was the house Henry Spangler and his family lived in near Emmitsburg Road or Willoughby's Run?

> *(Answer) Emmitsburg Road*

102. Was the Forney Farm located near Oak Ridge or Cemetery Ridge?

(Answer) Oak Ridge

103. James Warfield was known by what trade?

(Answer) Blacksmith

104. True or False - George Weikert and Jacob Weikert who both owned farms close to one another, were brothers.

(Answer) False, they were distant cousins.

105. At the Jacob Humelbaugh House which was used as a headquarters and hospital during the battle, what famous Confederate General died there and was also temporarily buried there?

(Answer) General William Barksdale

106. Which division commander at Gettysburg would be the last surviving full ranking General?

(Answer) General Adelbert Ames who died in 1933.

107. Which boy from Gettysburg was given the privilege of watering the horses and riding them to a stream, in Gamble's Brigade before the battle began?

(Answer) Leander Warren

108. When the Confederates invaded the town, whose house located on Seminary Ridge was especially targeted and ransacked. Why?

(Answer) Samuel Simon Schmucker was particularly targeted because of his anti-slavery views.

109. What did the Confederates do to Samuel Schmuckers water well in front of his house?

(Answer) The Confederates dropped amputated limbs from the hospital down the well to pollute the water.

110. On July 8, which Gettysburg citizen would discover wounded soldiers in the basement of the Lutheran

Seminary as it filled up with water potentially drowning them?

(Answer) Sarah Broadhead - With the help of a few others all the soldiers would be saved.

111. Who was Camp Letterman named after?

(Answer) Doctor Jonathan Letterman, Medical Director of the Army of the Potomac.

112. What farm was chosen for Camp Letterman?

(Answer) The George Wolf Farm

IN THIS SECTION **"Match the Patch"**

MATCH THE CORPS WITH THE INSIGNIA ASSOCIATED WITH IT

1) First Corps	A) Diamond
2) Second Corps	B) 5-Pointed Star
3) Third Corps	C) Sphere or Circle
4) Fifth Corps	D) Straight / Greek Cross
5) Sixth Corps	E) Clover Leaf or Trefoil
6) Eleventh Corps	F) Crescent Moon
7) Twelfth Corps	G) Maltese Cross

(Answers) (1 - C) (2 - E) (3 - A) (4 - G) (5 - D) (6 - F) (7 - B)

2) How were Divisions designated in a Corps?

    (Answer) By color of Corps emblem.

    First - Red / Second - White / Third - Blue

3) Given the Person **"Name the Patch" / Corps Insignia and Color**

    Example - Brigadier General James Wadsworth

    Answer : Sphere - Red - First Division

A 1) Brigadier General Henry Baxter

    Sphere - White - First Corps Second Division

B 2) Colonel William Tilton

    Maltese Cross - Red - Fifth Corps First Division

C 3) Colonel Charles Coster

    Crescent Moon - White - Eleventh Corps Second Division

D 4) Brigadier General Adelbert Ames

    Crescent Moon - Red - Eleventh Corps First Division

E 5) Brigadier General George Sears Greene

    Star - White - Twelfth Corps Second Division

F   6) Brigadier General Charles Graham

    Diamond - Red   -   Third Corps First Division

G   7) Colonel William McCandless

    Maltese Cross   -   Blue   -   Fifth Corps Third Division

H   8) Colonel Patrick Kelly

    Clover Leaf -   Red   -   Second Corps First Division

I   9) Major Ellis Spear

    Maltese Cross   -   Red   -   Fifth Corps First Division

J   10) Captain Francis Irsch

    Crescent Moon   -   Blue   -   Eleventh Corps Third Division

K   11) Colonel A.Van Horne Ellis

    Diamond -   Red   -   Third Corps First Division

L   12) Brigadier General Evander Law

No Patch, he was Confederate

M   13) Brigadier General George Stannard

Sphere - Blue - First Corps Third Division

N   14) Colonel Archibald McDougall

5-pointed Star - Red - Twelfth Corps First Division

O   15) Sergeant "Buster" Kilrain

No Badge - Fictional character in the movie "Gettysburg"

P   16) Color Sergeant Ben Crippen

Sphere - Blue - First Corps Third Division

Q   17) Lieutenant Colonel Douglas Fowler

Crescent Moon - Red - Eleventh Corps First Division

R   18) Lieutenant Colonel Franklin Sawyer

Clover Leaf - Blue - Second Corps Third Division

S 19) Colonel Philip Brown

Crescent Moon   -   Blue   -   Eleventh Corps Third Division

WHO AM I

I purchased a new farm around 1842 with my wife Mary on the Emmitsburg Road in Gettysburg. I was elected to the ministry in 1853. I started to sell peaches on a commercial basis and became well known for my canned peaches and dried fruit. On July 2, my family and I were ordered out of our home, when we returned our barn was burnt to the ground and my house was hit by seven shells. Everything inside was strewn about with blood everywhere.

For years after the battle, I would give listeners a sample of my peaches and tell them stories of those days.

Who Am I?

Reverend Joseph Sherfy

I was twenty-seven years old at the time of the battle. I lived with my grandparents Peter and Susan. On July 2, I prepared food for the Union soldiers stationed around our house when the shooting started. I cared for the wounded on July 2 and on July 3 and believe I may have saved some lives. After the war, the 1st Massachusetts Infantry paid my expenses to return to Gettysburg for the monument dedication and they even gave me a gold badge at the ceremony. Mr. Tipton took a photograph of me with my stove.

Who Am I?

Josephine Miller

I resided in the area of 126 Baltimore Street. I was very active whenever we had a Democratic election victory. I died in 1855 due to someone not knowing what an overcharge is when loading a cannon. I was buried at that same address. During the battle I received many a blank stare by both Union and Confederate troops.

Who Am I?

Penelope the Cannon

I was born in 1827 in New York City. I became a lawyer in New York City and later moved to California. On a voyage to Hawaii, King Kamehameha III appointed me head of the Hawaiian Navy which had no warships. During the war I joined the 71st New York State militia and in 1862 I was promoted to a newly raised New York infantry regiment as the Colonel. I nicknamed them the "Orange Blossoms". At Gettysburg, we were posted on Houcks Ridge and I was shot while on horseback urging my men to "stand firm".

Who Am I?

Augustus Van Horne Ellis

I was born in Germany in 1829. I was educated at the University of Bonn and started the paper "Bonner Zeitung" and was considered a revolutionary. I came to America and settled in Pennsylvania, then to Wisconsin. I started to speak on behalf of Lincoln, using German to raise his popularity among German American voters. I was made ambassador to Spain, quietly dissuading Spain from supporting the South. At Gettysburg, I was a Division Commander under

Oliver O. Howard. My wife and her sister helped establish the Kindergarten system in America.

Who Am I?

Carl Schurz

HOW DID YOU DO? LEVEL 2

(A) **If you answered 14 questions or less incorrectly**

<u>Rank</u> - Brigadier General

> GREAT JOB SIR, WE HAVE YOUR HEADQUAR-
> TERS SET UP IN THAT BIG HOUSE. HURRY, IT'S
> STARTING TO RAIN!

(B) **If you answered 36 or less questions incorrectly**

<u>Rank</u> - Colonel

> GOOD JOB, COLONEL. YOUR TENT IS ALL SET
> UP. HURRY, IT'S STARTING TO RAIN!

(C) **If you answered 37 or more incorrectly**

<u>Rank</u> - Private

> PRIVATE, YOU HAVE TO HIT THOSE BOOKS.
> KEEP TRYING.
>
> OH! NO. IT'S POURING CATS AND DOGS AND
> YOU'RE STILL ONLY HOLDING ONE HALF OF A
> TENT......GOOD LUCK!

Maryland State Memorial

LEVEL 3

PRE-BATTLE

1. Name the order of the top six Generals next in line to take command of the Army of the Potomac when General Hooker was relieved.

(Answer) 1. Henry Slocum   4. George Meade

2. John Sedgwick   5. Oliver Howard

3. John Reynolds   6. Dan Sickles

2. What local cavalry unit comprised of approximately fifty locals without uniforms, would join the militia defending Gettysburg?

(Answer) Captain Robert Bell's Adams County Cavalry Company.

3. Before locking up the troops of the captured militia in the courthouse on June 26, what does General Jubal Early tell them in an angry rant?

   (Answer) "You boys ought to be home with your mothers and not out in the fields where it is dangerous and you might get hurt!!."

4. Name General Buford's three Brigade Commanders.

   (Answer) General Wesley Merritt, Colonel Thomas Devin, Colonel William Gamble

5. What road did General Buford's cavalry columns enter into Gettysburg?

   (Answer) Emmitsburg Road

<u>July 1</u>

6. What two Confederate infantry companies suffered 100% casualties at Gettysburg?

> *(Answer) Company F 26th North Carolina, Company A 11th Mississippi.*

7. Which Union Brigade of the First Corps had the distinction of being the first infantry unit to reach the battlefield?

> *(Answer) The Second Brigade of the First Division under Brigadier General Lysander Cutler.*

8. What regiment, in its first battle, made a gallant stand north of the Railroad Cut on McPherson's Ridge, helping to save Hall's 2nd Maine Battery from capture?

> *(Answer) The 147th New York*

9. Which Colonel of the 7th Indiana disobeyed orders when he marched his men towards the sounds of battle instead of guarding the ammunition and supply trains?

(Answer) Colonel Ira Grover

10. When Confederate General Joseph Davis led his Brigade on July 1, his most experienced regiment was left behind to guard the division trains. Name the regiment.

(Answer) 11th Mississippi

11. What error did the Commander of the 76th New York make upon the approach of the 2nd Mississippi?

(Answer) Though his men fell by the second, he had his troops hold their fire because he could not identify the enemy because of the tall wheat - he thought they might be friendly troops.

12. Standing 6 feet 7 inches tall, General Solomon Meredith was known by what nickname?

(Answer) "Long Sol"

13. What brigade did Solomon Meredith command?

(Answer) The Iron Brigade

14. Was Solomon Meredith wounded at Gettysburg and if so, what part of his body?

>*(Answer) Yes, he was wounded. He was struck in the head by a shell fragment. His leg was crushed by his horse who was shot out from under him.*

15. Was Solomon Meredith respected as a Brigade Commander by his men?

>*(Answer) No, many grumbled about his lack of ability.*

16. On July 1, the flag of the 24th Michigan was carried in succession by ten soldiers. All but one was killed or

wounded. When Colonel Murrow saw the flag fall and grabbed it, a Private said " The Colonel of the 24th shall never carry the flag while I'm alive!" and sadly he was killed upon taking possession. Who was he?

(Answer) Private William Kelly

17. Confederate Private William Murphy, the flag bearer of the 2nd Mississippi recalled "how Union soldier after Union soldier tried to take the flag from me but were shot down". Who would eventually take the flag and earn the Congressional Medal of Honor for this feat?

(Answer) Corporal Francis Waller

18. When Colonel Rufus Dawes yelled to the Confederates in the railroad cut "throw down your muskets, where is the Colonel of this regiment?" Who stepped forward and handed Colonel Dawes his sword and surrendered his men?

(Answer) Major John Blair, 2nd Mississippi

19. After the surrender of the 225 men of the 2nd Mississippi in the railroad cut to the 6th Wisconsin, how many of its officers' swords was Rufus Dawes holding?

(Answer) Seven

20. Who was Union General Abner Doubleday referring to when he later wrote " I relied greatly upon his brigade, to hold the post assigned them...in truth, the key-point of the first day's battle".

(Answer) Colonel Roy Stone

21. When Colonel Roy Stone went down with wounds to the hip and arm, what Colonel of what regiment took command of the brigade?

(Answer) Colonel Langhorne Wister of the 150th Penn

22. What action would have General Baxter placing Colonel Wheelock under arrest after the slaughter of Iverson's men?

(Answer) He waved the flag of the 20th North Carolina defiantly and refused to take it to the rear for safekeeping when General Baxter ordered him to do so.

23. After General Baxter ordered Colonel Wheelock arrested for not bringing the flag of the 20th North Carolina to the rear, what other action did he do to further infuriate the Confederates?

(Answer) Colonel Wheelock ran his saber through the flag of the 20th North Carolina and twirled the flag around his sword.

24. How many flags would Baxter's Brigade take that afternoon?

(Answer) Four flags

25. What Confederate regiment would break through the Union line at the Seminary and cause the Union line to begin to collapse and flee through town?

(Answer) The 1st South Carolina Volunteers

26. Who commanded the Brigade that broke the Union line at the Seminary?

    (Answer) Colonel Abner Perrin, South Carolina

27. Colonel Perrin's advancing Brigade was exposed to enfilading fire by the tactical mistake of what Confederate Brigade Commander during its advance upon the Union line at the Seminary?

    (Answer) Brigadier General James Lane

28. Colonel Perrin was in temporary command of the South Carolina Brigade because its commander had been wounded at Chancellorsville. Who was this injured officer?

    (Answer) Brigadier General Samuel McGowen

29. What two regiments were detached from the Confederate Brigade of Colonel Edward O'Neal and

therefore were not part of the assault by that Brigade from Oak Hill?

(Answer) The 3rd Alabama and 5th Alabama

30. What reason did Colonel O'Neal give for not moving forward and supervising his brigade's movements instead of remaining with his reserve regiment?

(Answer) When he gave the order, he realized he and his staff did not have horses.

31. General Alfred Iverson's Brigade lost sixty-five percent at Gettysburg, what other Confederate Brigade Commander would also lose sixty-five percent of his brigade at Gettysburg?

(Answer) General Richard Garnett

32. After the Battle of Gettysburg, what action did the men in General Alfred Iverson's Brigade take?

(Answer) They refused to serve under him.

33. When Captain Francis Irsch and four companies of the 45th New York were under fire near the McLean Farm by the 5th Alabama and Page's Battery, what Union Artillery Commander would fire into Page's Battery causing them to withdraw as well as pouring canister into O'Neal's left flank?

(Answer) Captain Hubert Dilger

34. Which Union Eleventh Corps regiment marched farther than any regiment out on the Carlisle Road and fired into the flank of the 44th GA?

(Answer) The 157th New York

35. The 157th NY was engaged with the Confederates which formed a semi-circle around them. Did General Schimmelfennig communicate a retreat effectively?

(Answer) No, one of his aides "hollered" from a distance to retreat, but nobody from the 157th heard or saw the aide of Schimmelfennig.

36. Who was the Colonel of the 157th New York, whose regiment suffered terrible losses along the Carlisle Road July 1?

(*Answer*) *Colonel Philip Brown*

37. What percentage loss did the 157th New York suffer?

(*Answer*) *Seventy-five per cent*

38. During the fighting on Blocher's Knoll, this Union battery commander was shot in the leg below the knee then amputated his own leg with a pocket knife. Who was he?

(*Answer*) *Lieutenant Bayard Wilkeson*

39. Would Lieutenant Wilkeson survive the battle of Gettysburg?

(*Answer*) *Sadly, he would not.*

40. After Lieutenant Wilkeson went down, who took charge of the battery and maintained fire on the Confederates?

(Answer) Lt. Eugene Bancroft

41. As Colonel Issac Avery's North Carolina Brigade approached Coster's position near the brickyard, who benefited more by the topography of the area-Coster's men or Avery's men?

(Answer) Avery's North Carolina Brigade

42. Of the two New York regiments of Coster's Brigade, the 134th NY and the 154th NY, which one lost its colors during the retreat through town?

(Answer) Neither, both flags were saved.

43. During the battle, a Lieutenant Colonel of the 82nd Illinois pointed out a sign to General Oliver Howard in the cemetery grounds that read "driving, riding and shooting on these grounds is strictly prohibited and any person violating this ordinance will be punished by fine

or imprisonment." A shell then hit the sign and smashed it to pieces. What was General Howard's response?

(Answer) "Well, the ordinance is rescinded, I think the battle can go on."

July 2

44. Which Union regiment supported the 1st United States Sharpshooters in Pitzers Woods on July 2?

    (Answer) The 3rd Maine

45. In the Triangular Field, once the 1st Texas advanced to the stone wall, why was Captain Smith's Artillery ineffective defending itself?

    (Answer) The Artillery was unable to depress their guns sufficiently.

46. With tears in his eyes, Captain Smith pleaded with the 124th N.Y. upon the advance of the 1st Texas up the Triangular Field. What did he say?

    (Answer) "For God's sake men, don't let them take my guns away from me!!"

47. How many guns did Captain Smith use firing into the Confederates in the Triangular Field on Houck's Ridge?

(Answer) Four

48. How many guns did Captain Smith hold in reserve?

    (Answer) Two

49. What sight did the soldiers of the 124th New York witness as one angry soldier recalled "We turned into wild beasts"?

    (Answer) The sight of their beloved Major Cromwell shot and killed while on horseback.

50. Which two Confederate Regiments fighting the 124th New York in the Triangular Field would capture Captain Smith's four guns?

    (Answer) The 1st Texas and 15th Georgia

51. During the battle on July 2, what Confederate regiment chased Union skirmishers from the Weikert's Farm (today's Timber's Farm)?

(Answer) The 3rd Arkansas

52. After the 3rd Arkansas chased out the Union skirmishers and moved forward, what Union regiment in the Wheatfield fired upon them?

(Answer) 17th Maine

53. Because of the noise in the Wheatfield, Colonel John Brooke ordered his brigade forward. Realizing they could not hear him, he grabbed the colors from what regiment in his brigade and carried it forward?

(Answer) The 53rd Pennsylvania

54. After General Zook took a mortal wound to the abdomen, who would take command of the brigade?

(Answer) Colonel Charles Freudenburg of the 52nd New York

55. In his official report, was General Kershaw pleased or angry with General Barksdale during the attack on July 2?

(Answer) Angry, he said "This Brigade (Barksdale)
then moved so far to the left as to no longer
afford me any assistance."

56. On July 2 at 4:00 P.M. General Edward Johnson ordered Major Joseph Latimore to deploy artillery on what hill?

(Answer) Benners Hill

57. Would Major Joseph Latimore be successful after opening fire on the enemy's position?

(Answer) No, a swift and devastating reaction from
Union batteries would silence his guns.

58. After a terrible wound to his right arm, Major Latimore was being carried off the field. What did he ask his men to do?

(Answer) "Fight harder and avenge my loss."

59. How many times was the flag and staff of the 149th New York hit by enemy fire and who mended the broken staff

with leather straps and wood from an ammunition box while the battle raged?

(Answer) It was hit 88 times, and it was mended by Color Sergeant William Lilly.

60. At 9:00 P.M. on July 2, Colonel James Rice asked Colonel Chamberlain of the 20th Maine to move up Big Round Top and clear it. What brigade was ordered to clear Big Round Top earlier but was reluctant to do so?

(Answer) The Brigade of Colonel James Fisher (Crawford's Division)

July 3

61. How many regiments did General George Pickett have in his division and from what states did these regiments hail?

    (Answer) 15 regiments - all from Virginia.

62. What are two possible reasons why the Confederate artillery was so inaccurate and overshot the Union infantry and artillery near the Stone Wall on Cemetery Ridge?

    (Answer) 1) Heavy smoke made it hard to judge distance.

    2) Constant recoil of the guns dug deep trails in the ground throwing off aim.

    3) Fuses were not from the Richmond Armory but from Charleston Armory and were slower burning thus artillery crews miscalculated lengths.

63. Which Confederate regiment that participated in Picketts Charge had also been in the western theater at Fort Donelson?

(Answer) The 56ᵗʰ Virginia

64. Which one of the three brigades in General George Picketts Division did General James Longstreet command at First Manassas?

(Answer) Kemper's Brigade

65. During Pickett's Charge, Colonel Robert Allen witnessing many of his color bearers go down, he picked up the flag and he would soon go down with a mortal wound. He was commanding what Confederate regiment?

(Answer) 28th Virginia

66. What regiment of Colonel David Lang's (Perry's Brigade) would take the majority of the flanking fire from the 16th Vermont?

(Answer) The 2nd Florida

67. What four regiments comprised the Philadelphia Brigade?

(Answer) 69th, 71st, 72nd and 106th Pennsylvania

68. The Philadelphia Brigades popular General Owen was replaced by General Alexander Webb, a spit and polish "West Pointer". Can you name two incidents that made his men resent him?

> *(Answer) 1) General Webb made his officers wear their shoulder boards and other accouterments of rank that they had discarded.*
> *2) He told his men "I will shoot any stragglers like dogs."*
> *3) Before the battle, he refused to allow his men to remove their shoes and socks fording Monocacy Creek.*

69. True or False - General John Gibbon had two brothers that served in the Confederacy.

(Answer) False - General Gibbon had three brothers serve in the Confederacy.

70. What Lieutenant had his sword taken away before Pickett's Charge for disobeying an order to find his thirsty men water, so he carried a camp hatchet into the battle as a weapon.

(Answer) Lieutenant Stephen Brown of the 13th Vermont

71. General Armistead would take a group of about one hundred Confederates across the wall of the Angle. What Union regiment would then pour fire into them?

(Answer) 72nd Pennsylvania

72. How many times was General Armistead hit by enemy fire?

(Answer) Twice, he was shot in the arm and the leg.

73. Union Captain Bingham would assist a wounded General Armistead, both members of the Masonic Order of Freemasons. What other brigade commander under General George Pickett was also a Freemason?

(Answer) General James Kemper

74. The 13th Vermont fought gallantly on July 3rd by flanking Kempers Brigade as it approached the copse of trees. What would happen to this regiment on July 21, 1863?

(Answer) It would be mustered out of service.

75. True or False - John Bachelder refused to allow a twelve-foot monument dedicated to General George Pickett.

(Answer) True

76. When General Lee reads the report of General Pickett after the battle, he instructs General Pickett to do what?

(Answer) Rewrite and resubmit it.

77. Does General Pickett comply with General Lee's instructions?

(Answer) No.

MONUMENTS

78. What regiment numbering only 75 men has five memorials for its service on July 2 in the Wheatfield?

(Answer) 27th Connecticut

79. What does each of the five faces of the soldiers on the North Carolina Memorial symbolize?

(Answer) Pain, Determination, Fear, Encouragement and Pride.

80. The Regimental monument to the 4th Ohio on East Cemetery Hill is composed of what material?

(Answer) White bronze

81. From 1978 to 1988, what was atop the Eternal Light Peace Memorial?

    (Answer) A sodium vapor electrical light.

82. How are General Robert E. Lee and General George G. Meade similar on their respective statues?

    (Answer) Both Generals have removed their hats.

83. What artist created the equestrian statues of Generals John F. Reynolds, George G. Meade, John Sedgwick and the bust of Abraham Lincoln in the National Cemetery?

    (Answer) Henry Bush-Brown

84. He claimed to be the last Confederate veteran of the Civil War, dying on December 19, 1959 at the supposed age of 117. His name appears on the back of the Soldiers and Sailors Memorial of the Confederacy. Who was this man?

(Answer) Walter Washington Williams. (He lied about his age. He did not participate in the Civil War.)

85. Where on the battlefield would you find "Anchisauripus Sillimani"?

(Answer) The stone bridge over Plum Run at the base of Big Round Top; dinosaur footprints.

86. Devil's Den is composed of what type of rock?

(Answer) Igneous diabase.

87. The oldest known rock inscription on the battlefield is located where and what is the inscription?

(Answer) The Elephant Rock at Devil's Den, reading, "D Forney 1849".

88. Why did George W. Warner unveil the 20th Connecticut's monument by having a rope tied around his waist?

(Answer) He had lost both his arms during the battle.

89. What is the number of the gun barrel at the base of General Buford's statue, which fired the first Union artillery shot of the battle?

    (Answer) #233

90. What marks the spot on Barlow's Knoll, where Colonel Douglas Fowler of the 17th Connecticut Regiment was killed?

    (Answer) A flagpole

91. What two insects are depicted on the Masonic Memorial in the Gettysburg National Cemetery?

    (Answer) A butterfly and a horsefly.

92. What inscription from the speech of Edward Everett delivered at the National Cemetery dedication, is engraved on the Minnesota Urn in the National Cemetery?

(Answer) "All time is the millenium of their glory".

93. What woman's name is carved on the breech of one of the cannon tubes of the 9th Massachusetts Battery, located at the Trostle Farm?

    (Answer) "Cora"

94. What Indian Chief is depicted on the 42nd New York Regimental Monument on Hancock Avenue?

    (Answer) Chief Tammand of the Lenape Tribe.

95. Finish this quote from the Massachusetts Sharpshooters Monument on Hancock Avenue.

    (Answer) "In God we put our trust, but ...... "kept our powder dry."

96. What is the only statue on the battlefield which can be seen in the movie, "Gettysburg"?

(Answer) Statue of General G. K. Warren on Little Round Top.

97. What two Union regiments have the most monuments on the battlefield, a total of five each?

(Answer) 95th New York and the 27th Connecticut

98. The Gaelic slogan on the 28th Massachusetts Regimental monument, "Faugh A Ballaugh" means what?

(Answer) "Clear the way"

99. At the base of the National Soldier's Monument in the Gettysburg National Cemetery, stands a smaller memorial with President Lincoln's Gettysburg Address engraved upon it. What state erected this memorial?

(Answer) The state of Kentucky - to honor Kentucky's native son.

GETTYSBURG ADDRESS / CEMETERY

100. Name the first copy of the Gettysburg Address.

   (Answer) Nicolay copy

101. Name the second copy of the Gettysburg Address.

   (Answer) Hay copy

102. Name the third copy of the Gettysburg Address.

   (Answer) Everett copy

103. And the fourth and fifth copies.

   (Answer) (fourth) Bancroft Copy, and (fifth) Bliss copy

104. On November 18, 1863 on the eve of the Gettysburg Address, David Wills held a dinner party reception in honor of President Lincoln. How many guests did he have?

(Answer) Thirty-eight

105. During the Wills dinner party, what military band serenaded President Lincoln from the large Public Square?

(Answer) 5th New York Artillery Band

106. What Colonel outraged by some in the crowd said "I'm offended that the President had not been received well - you owe your country - you owe your name as American citizens".

(Answer) Colonel John Furney of Furney War Press

107. Secretary of State William Seward, President Lincoln's closest advisor, came to Gettysburg as well. Where did he stay?

(Answer) In the home of Robert Harper

108. Who are the <u>two</u> African Americans soldiers from the Civil War buried in the Gettysburg National Cemetery?

(Answer) Private Henry Gooden - 127th U.S. Colored Troops Private Charles Parker, 115th U.S. Colored Troops

109. Did Major General Charles Collis, buried with the 114th Pennsylvania in the Soldiers National Cemetery, fight with the 114th at the Battle of Gettysburg?

(Answer) No, he could not due to illness.

110. President Richard Nixon's great-grandfather, Private George Nixon would see action at Gettysburg with the 73rd Ohio and later be buried in the National Cemetery, Row C, #4. What drummer of the 73rd crawled to an injured Nixon shot in the hip, put him on his back and crawled back to Union lines?

(Answer) Twenty year old Drummer Richard Enderlin

111. Who would become one of the first matrons of the "Orphans Homestead" located on Baltimore Street? Her husband would be buried in the Soldiers National Cemetery only yards away.

(Answer) Philanda Humiston, the widow of Amos Humiston, 154th New York

112. What is unique about the grave of Private Orin Walker, 20th Maine Infantry, Row E, #4 in The Soldiers National Cemetery?

    (Answer) Although suffering a horrific wound, he would survive the war and live for another 20 years. The identity of the body in that grave remains a mystery.

113. During the battle, a Sergeant from the 23rd Pennsylvania Infantry previously killed at Fair Oaks had his headstone damaged by the artillery fire from the battle. Whose grave is this?

    (Answer) Sergeant Frederick Huber (It is not repaired as of this day.)

114. Who was the bodyguard for President Lincoln at Gettysburg at the time of the Gettysburg Address?

(Answer) H. P. Bigham

115. What sight was amusing to some in the crowd when President Lincoln mounted his horse for the parade to Cemetery Hill?

   (Answer) President Lincoln's six feet 4 inch stature upon his horse. His legs nearly touched the ground.

116. On November 19 at the start of the consecration program, who opened it with a solemn prayer which brought many to tears?

   (Answer) Reverend T. H. Stockton, the Chaplain of the U.S. Senate

GENERALS AND WEST POINT

117. What five Union Generals would be killed at Gettysburg?

> *(Answer) 1) General John Reynolds*
>
> > *2) General Elon Farnsworth*
> >
> > *3) General Strong Vincent (promoted on his deathbed)*
> >
> > *4) General Stephen Weed*
> >
> > *5) General Samuel Zook*

118. Name the four youngest Union Generals at Gettysburg.

> *(Answer) Adelbert Ames - 27 years*
> > *Judson Kilpatrick - 27 years*
> >
> > *Elon Farnsworth - 25 years*
> >
> > *George Custer - 23 years*

119. Name the three oldest Union Generals at Gettysburg?

> *(Answer) George S. Green - 62 years*
> > *James Barnes - 61 years*
> >
> > *Lysander Cutler - 56 years*

120. At the battle, who was older, General William Barksdale or General Jubal Early?

(Answer) Jubal Early was forty-six years old, General Barksdale was only forty one years old.

121. Who was the older General, John Sedgwick or Thomas Rowley during the Battle of Gettysburg?

(Answer) Thomas Rowley - fifty-four years old, John Sedgwick was forty-nine years old.

122. What year did James Longstreet graduate from West Point?

(Answer) 1842

123. Out of a class of 56, what was Longstreet's class rank at West Point?

(Answer) 54 out of 56

124. What year did Robert E. Lee graduate from West Point?

(Answer) Class of 1829 / Second out of a class of forty-six

125. What Union General at Gettysburg graduated fifth in the 1829 class of West Point, three places from Robert E. Lee?

(Answer) General James Barnes

126. General George Pickett graduated last in his Class of 1846. What Confederate General graduated last in 1847?

(Answer) Major General Harry Heth last out of a class of 38.

127. In 1862, what two West Point engineers at Gettysburg graduated first and second out of a class of 28?

(Answer) Lt. Ronald McKenzie - First out of a class of 28.
Lt. George Gillespie - Second out of a class of 28

TOWN

128. True or False - The Springs Hotel near Willoughby Run was used as a Union Hospital after the battle.

    (Answer) False - The hotel was built in 1869.

129. In what harness makers cellar did Sarah Broadhead and her four year old daughter hide during the beginning of the Battle?

    (Answer) David Troxel's cellar

130. Catherine Trostle came back to her home to find it ransacked and used as a hospital and dead horses left rotting on her property. Where was her husband at this time?

    (Answer) In an insane asylum.

131. What ten year old girl was deputized as a nurse with her first assignment assisting a doctor in an amputation?

(Answer) Sadie Bushman.

132. True or False - An amusement park was built on Cemetery Ridge in the years following the battle.

    (Answer) True, it was called Fantasy Land.

133. True or False - Classes were in session at the start of the Battle on July 1, 1863.

    (Answer) True.

134. All visitors to the Battlefield are asked to show respect and follow all Park Service rules. What one rock is forbidden to walk on and has a sign on it which reminds all visitors.

    (Answer) The Warren Rock on Little Round Top.

135. What year did the re-interment of the Confederate dead at Gettysburg begin?

    (Answer) 1872

136. After the battle, this Gettysburg African American woman hired a horse and wagon and would spend her life savings on food and clothing helping the wounded soldiers, Union and Confederate alike. Who was she?

(Answer) Lydia Hamilton Smith

137. Name the six trolley cars named after Corps Commanders at Tipton's Gettysburg Electric Railway.

(Answer)   *1. Hancock   4. Sedgwick*

            2. Howard   5. Sickles

            3. Reynolds   6. Slocum

138. A Civil War Zouave uniform was modeled after what foreign army?

(Answer) Zouave uniforms were modeled after North Africa's French Colonial Army.

139. What was a Vivandiere?

(Answer) It was a female in a Zouave regiment, dressed in similar clothing to men and performed a variety of duties, most notably nursing the wounded on the battlefield.

140. What famous Vivandiere accompanied the 114th Pennsylvania to Gettysburg?

(Answer) Mary Tepee or French Mary

REGIMENTAL NICKNAME

(Match the Regiment to the Nickname)

1)	20th Massachusetts	A)	Corn Exchange Regiment
2)	105th Pennsylvania	B)	2nd Bucktails
3)	149th Pennsylvania	C)	Harvard Regiment
4)	40th New York	D)	California Regiment
5)	118th Pennsylvania	E)	Boston Volunteers
6)	12th New Hampshire	F)	Mountaineers
7)	45th New York	G)	Lockiel Cameron Highlanders
8)	71st Pennsylvania	H)	Wildcats
9)	11th Massachusetts	I)	Pee Dee Guards
10)	78th New York	J)	German Rifles 5th Regiment
11)	23rd North Carolina	K)	Mozart Regiment

1 - C	7 - J
2 - H	8 - D
3 - B	9 - E
4 - K	10 - G
5 - A	11 - I
6 - F	

MORE REGIMENTAL NICKNAMES

1)	20th Indiana	A)	Henry Wilson Regiment
2)	44th New York	B)	Cincinnati Regiment
3)	12th New Jersey	C)	Collis Zouaves
4)	22nd Massachusetts	D)	Ellsworth's Avengers
5)	124th New York	E)	Baxters Fire Zouaves
6)	5th Ohio	F)	Hardtack Regiment
7)	114th Pennsylvania	G)	Fighting 300
8)	72nd Pennsylvania	H)	Paddy Owens Regiment
9)	154th New York	I)	Orange Blossoms
10)	69th Pennsylvania	J)	Extra Billy Smiths Boys
11)	49th Virginia	K)	Buck and Ball Regiment

1 - G   *7 - C*

2 - D   *8 - E*

3 - K   *9 - F*

4 - A   *10 - H*

5 - I   *11 - J*

6 - B

NAME THE ROAD

Match the Monument to the Road

1. 90th Pennsylvania Infantry

2. South Carolina State Memorial

3. Excelsior Brigade Memorial

4. 1st Delaware Infantry

5. Texas State Memorial

6. 149th Pennsylvania Infantry

7. 53rd Pennsylvania Infantry

8. 5th New Hampshire Infantry

9. 149th New York Infantry

10. 2nd Massachusetts Infantry

A. South Confederate Avenue

B. Brooke Avenue

C. Ayers Avenue

D. Doubleday Avenue

E. Baltimore Pike

F. Sickles Avenue

G. North Slocum Avenue

H. West Confederate Avenue

I. Wright Avenue

J. Carman Avenue

11. 21st Pernnsylvania Cavalry   K. Hancock Avenue

12. 20th Maine Infantry   L. Warren Avenue

13. 38 Pennsylvania Infantry   M. Chambersburg Pike

14. 26th North Carolina Infantry   N. Meredith Avenue

15. John Burns Portrait Statue   O. Stone Avenue

16. 45th New York Infantry   P. Reynolds Avenue

17. Abner Doubleday Portrait Statue   Q. Howard Avenue

18. 15th and 50th New York Engineers   R. Crawford Avenue

19. 83rd Pennsylvania Infantry   S. Wheatfield Road

20. 114th Pennsylvania   T. Sedgwick Avenue

U. Sykes Avenue

V. Pleasonton Avenue

W. Emmitsburg Road

Answers

1 - D	*11 - E*
2 - H	*12 - I*
3 - F	*13 - L*
4 - K	*14 - N*
5 - A	*15 - O*
6 - M	*16 - Q*
7 - B	*17 - P*
8 - C	*18 - V*
9 - G	*19 - U*
10 - J	*20 - W*

<u>NAME THE ROAD</u>

Match the Place to the Street

1.	St. Francis Xavier Church	A.	York Street
2.	Home of Jacob Weikert	B.	Middle Street
3.	Lutheran Theological Seminary	C.	Hanover Road
4.	Home of Henry Culp	D.	Tanneytown Road
5.	Home of Salome Myers	E.	Baltimore Pike
6.	Daniel Lady Farm	F.	West High Street
7.	St. James Lutheran Church	G.	High Street
8.	Home of Catherine Snyder	H.	Hospital Road
9.	Home of George Bushman	I.	Chambersburg Street
10.	Christ Lutheran Church	J.	Seminary Ridge
11.	Home of Elias Sheads	K.	Table Rock Road
12.	Home of Henry Garlach	L.	Willoughby Run Road

13. Home of George Culp

M. Chambersburg Pike

14. Adams County Poor House (Farm)

N. Harrisburg Road

15. Home of Joseph Bayly

O. Baltimore Street

P. Carlisle Road

Answers

1. - G	9. - H
2. - D	10. - I
3. - J	11. - M
4. - B	12. - O
5. - F	13. - L
6. - C	14. - N
7. - A	15. - K
8. - E	

WHO AM I?

I was born in Maine but later moved to Bridgeport, Connecticut. I enlisted in a Connecticut regiment, and before the Battle of Gettysburg, we fought at Antietam, Fredericksburg and Chancellorsville.

After the cannons stopped firing on July 3rd, the Confederates charged up to the stone wall to our front. After much hand to hand fighting, I saw the colors of the 14th Tennessee unguarded about 50 yards away. With the help of two others, I ran to retrieve the colors. To my surprise, when I reached the flag, I found the Confederates lying around it. I yelled at the top of my lungs, waving my saber and then ran back to our lines with the flag. This earned me a Congressional Medal of Honor.

After the war, I was a successful banker in Connecticut and helped P.T. Barnum found the Barnum Museum in Bridgeport.

Who Am I?

Sergeant Major William B. Hincks

I was born in Ireland. I came to America as a boy and my family made our home in Philadelphia.

I was wounded during the charge up Marye's Heights, Fredericksburg and at Chancellorsville. I saved the guns of the 5th Maine and was awarded the Congressional Medal of Honor.

At Gettysburg on July 2, after hearing the Brigade Chaplain Father Corby pronounce the words of absolution, I led my regiment of Pennsylvanians into a dense wooded area and we fired into the enemy. Advancing, we were suddenly among them. I yelled "Confederates, lay down your arms". To my relief many did and were taken prisoner. I believe they were from South Carolina. We soon vacated Stony Hill back to the Taneytown Road and witnessed the cannonade and charge on that hot July 3. Many of the Irish can hold their heads high for what we did in the Wheatfield and Stony Hill at Gettysburg.

Who Am I?

Colonel St. Clair A. Mulholland

I was born in 1837 in Saxonburg, Pennsylvania. My father would start a very successful wire rope business in which I help manage as I went to school for Engineering. After listening to a speech by President Lincoln, I joined the Union Army. In time, I was used as an engineer at various battles. I would observe General Lee's advance into the North in a hot air balloon and report to General Meade.

I was present at Little Round Top as an aide to General G. K. Warren. Seeing the approach of Confederate General Hood's Division toward Little Round Top, General Warren and myself rushed to the rear of the hill, where I helped to lead the 140th New York Regiment, commanded by Colonel Patrick O'Rorke, back to the crest of the hill. After the war I would marry General Warren's sister, Emily. In the years that followed, I was Chief Engineer during the construction of one of the most famous bridges in New York.

Who Am I?

Washington Augustus Roebling (Brooklyn Bridge)

HOW DID YOU DO?

(Were you promoted?)

<u>LEVEL 3</u>

(A)   **15 or less questions answered incorrectly...**

<u>Rank</u> - Major General

GREAT JOB MAJOR GENERAL, YOU CERTAINLY ARE VERY WISE AND KNOWLEDGEABLE. DINNER IS SERVED! STEAK, HAM, APPLE PIE, COFFEE AND YOUR PIPE!!!

(B)   **40 or less answered incorrectly...**

<u>Rank</u> - Brigadier General

GOOD JOB BRIGADIER GENERAL, YOU SHOULD BE A MAJOR GENERAL IN

NO TIME!! DINNER IS SERVED!! FRIED CHICKEN, CORNBREAD AND

COFFEE.

(C) **41 or more answered incorrectly...**

<u>Rank</u> - Private

PRIVATE....YOU REALLY NEED TO HIT THOSE BOOKS BUT KEEP TRYING....

OH, BY THE WAY, I KNOW YOU WERE ON PICKET DUTY AND YOU MISSED CHOW, BUT YOU CAN HAVE THIS OLD PIECE OF HARDTACK AND THIS CONFEDERATE COFFEE I FOUND NEAR THE HORSES.....

Monument of the 73rd New York Infantry

(2nd Fire Zouaves)

REFERENCES USED FOR THIS BOOK AND SUGGESTED READING

Adelman, Garry E. and Timothy H. Smith.*Devils Den, A History and Guide*. Thomas Publications, Gettysburg, Pa 1977

Alexander, John and Jim Slade.*Firestorm at Gettysburg Civilian Voices, June-November 1863*. Schiffer Publishing Ltd., 2004

Bachelder, James B.*The Bachelder Papers, Volume I, II, III. Gettysburg in Their Own Words.*
Copyright- The New Hampshire Historical Society,
Published- Morningside House Inc.
Dayton, OH: 1994

Busey, John W. and David G. Martin. *Regimental Strengths and Losses at Gettysburg*.
Longstreet House, Hightstown, NJ: 1982

Coco, Gregory. *A Strange and Blighted LandGettysburg: The Aftermath of a Battle*.
Gettysburg, PA: Thomas Publications, 1995

Coddington, Edwin B. *The Gettysburg Campaign-A Study in Command*. Simon & Schuster Inc.
New York, 1968

Frampton, Roy E. and James M. Cole. *Lincoln and Human Interest Stories of the Gettysburg National Cemetery*.
Sheridan Press, Hanover, Pennsylvania, 1995

Gottfried, Bradley M. *Brigades of Gettysburg: The Union and Confederate Brigades atThe Battle of Gettysburg*. Da Capo Press, Cambridge, MA: 2002

Gottfried, Bradley M. *The Maps of Gettysburg: An Atlas of The Gettysburg Campaign*. Savas Beatie LLC, New York, 2007

Hawthorne, Frederick W. *Gettysburg - Stories of The Men and Monuments as Told by Battlefield Guides.* Published by The Association of Licensed Battlefield Guides, 1988

Hess, Earl, J. *Picketts Charge - The Last Attack at Gettysburg.* The University of North Carolina Press, 2001

Pfanz, Harry W. *GettysburgThe First Day.* The University of North Carolina Press, Chapel Hill, NC: 2001

Pfanz, Harry W. *GettysburgThe Second Day.* The University of North Carolina Press, Chapel Hill, NC: 1987

Sears, Stephen W. *Gettysburg.* Mariner Books, November 2004

Smith, Timothy H. *Farms at Gettysburg, The Fields of Battle.* Thomas Publications, Gettysburg, PA: 2007

Smith, Timothy H. *The Story of Lee's Headquarters.* Thomas Publications, Gettysburg, PA: 1995

Stackpole, Edward. *They Met at Gettysburg.* Mechanicsburg, PA: Stackpole Books, 1956

Trudeau, Andre Noah. *Gettysburg, A Testing of Courage.* Harper Collins Publishers, New York, 2002

United States War Department. *The War of The RebellionA Compilation of The Official Records of The Union and Confederate Armies.* Washington: Government Printing Office, 1800-1901

Williams, William G. *Days of Darkness, The Gettysburg Civilians.* White Mane Publishing, Shippensburg, PA: 1986

Files of the Adams County Historical Society

Files of the Gettysburg National Military Park

Breinigsville, PA USA
10 December 2010
251126BV00005B/34/P

9 781612 153636